190 years of

The
U. S. Western District of
Louisiana

1823-2013

Edited by Randy DeCuir

www.thelouisianapurchase.net

To Rodney and Tucker
Defenders of the constitution

Table of Contents

Section I

The history of
U. S. Western District of
Louisiana

HISTORY OF THE UNITED STATES DISTRICT COURT FOR THE WESTERN DISTRICT OF LOUISIANA

The constitution of the United States provides in Article III that "The judicial Power of the United States, shall be vested in one supreme Court, and in such inferior Courts as the Congress may from time to time ordain and establish."

The Western District federal court of Louisiana was originally established by the Congress in 1823, when the state federal court was divided into two districts, east and west.

Before the Western District was created, all of Louisiana was under one court, based in New Orleans.

In 1804, Congress had established a United States District Court in the Territory of Orleans. This was the first federal court in what today comprises the State of Louisiana. There was one judge, Dominic Augustin Hall of South Carolina. Hall, Louisiana's first federal judge, was nominated by President Thomas Jefferson. There have never been elections for the federal judiciary, as they have always been appointed by the sitting president. (State courts in Louisiana were originally appointed by the governor, but are now elected.)

When Louisiana became a state in 1812, Judge Hall then continued under the new name of U. S. District Court of the State of Louisiana until 1821, when he was replaced by Judge John Dick. Judge Dick, an Irish immigrant, had been nominated by President James Monroe.

In 1823, Congress divided the court into the two districts, the Eastern District of Louisiana and the Western District of Louisiana. Judge John Dick was authorized to sit in both districts.

He was succeeded in 1824 by Judge Thomas B. Robertson, who served through 1828. Robertson had been nominated by President James Monroe.

In 1829 Samuel H. Harper was nominated by President Andrew Jackson and appointed district judge. He served until 1841.

In 1841, Theodore H. McCaleb was nominated by President Tyler and appointed as district judge.

Prior to 1837, the federal courts in Louisiana were not assigned to a circuit court of appeal. In 1837, the Louisiana courts were assigned to the Ninth Circuit, and, in 1842, the Louisiana courts were reassigned to the Fifth Circuit, where they remain to this time.

In 1845, Congress combined the Eastern and Western Districts into a single court for the District of Louisiana. Judge Theodore H. McCaleb continued to serve as the single judge of the court.

Shreveport, Louisiana

***U.S. Post Office and Court House, pictured in 1900, Completed in
1887. Architect: N.S. Allen. The U.S. District Court for the
Western District of Louisiana met here until 1910; the U.S. Circuit
Court for the Western District of Louisiana met here until 1910.
The building was razed in 1910.***

In 1849, Congress re-divided the court into the Eastern and
Western Districts. A new judgeship was created for the
Western District of Louisiana. President Zachary Taylor
nominated Henry Boyce of Rapides Parish, who was the

second Irish immigrant to be appointed district judge for the Western District of Louisiana. He served until he resigned in February of 1861, when Louisiana seceded from the United States to join the Confederate States of America.

During the Civil War, only the New Orleans area was under the United States flag, but was under the martial law control of the U. S. Army.

In 1866 after the conclusion of the Civil War, Congress once again joined the two districts into a single district for the State of Louisiana with one authorized judgeship. Edward Henry Durell, who had been appointed by President Abraham Lincoln before the war in the Eastern District, was appointed judge of the combined districts. Durell served until 1874.when he was replaced by Edward Coke Billings, who had been nominated by President Ulysses S. Grant.

In 1881, Congress once again divided the court and established the present Western District of Louisiana with one authorized judgeship. Alexander Boarman, a Confederate veteran Captain, was appointed as district judge for the court and served until 1916. He was nominated by President James Garfield.

During Judge Boarman's tenure, new Courthouse buildings were constructed at five locations within the Western District: Shreveport (1887), Opelousas (1891), Monroe (1892), Alexandria (1896), and Lake Charles (1912). During the span of his career, Judge Boarman, as the only judge in the district, traveled by train, steamboat, and finally automobile to the various locations to hold court.

Two of these five courthouse buildings were used until the 1930s, when Roosevelt era WPA buildings were built to replace them in Alexandria and Monroe. The Opelousas building was used the longest, housing court until 1967. The Lake Charles courthouse was in use until 1960. The Shreveport Courthouse had the shortest life, it was replaced in 1912.

The Federal Building in Monroe, completed in 1892, used till 1933 In 1892 the U.S. Court House and Post Office was completed in Monroe., under Supervising Architects: James H. Windrim and Willoughby J. Edbrooke Traveling judges met here until 1933; the Federal Circuit Court for the Western District of Louisiana also met here until that court was abolished in 1912. The building was razed in 1965.

Federal Courthouse, Alexandria, completed in 1896. Used until 1933.

Shreveport's U.S. Post Office and Court House, Completed in 1912. Seen during construction. Architect: James Knox Taylor. In 1931, a Fourth upper floor was added under Architect James A.

***U.S. Post Office and Courthouse in Lake Charles, Completed in
1912. Supervising Architect: James Knox Taylor The U.S. District
Court for the Western District of Louisiana met here until 1959.
Now privately owned.***

In 1917, George Whitfield Jack was appointed district judge
and served until 1924. Jack was the first Louisiana native to
be appointed to the Western District, all of his predecessor
having come from other states and nations. Not only was Jack
born in the state, but he was also born within the Western
Distirct, in Natchitoches.

In 1924, Benjamin C. Dawkins, Sr. was appointed as judge of
the court and served until 1953.

The 1912 Shreveport Federal building after the fourth floor was added in 1931, The Court met here until 1974.

U.S. Post Office and Court House, 515 Murray Street, Alexandria, completed in 1933, Art Deco Style. Architect: Edward F. Neild. Still in use by the U.S. District Court for the Western District of

U.S. Post Office and Court House at Monroe (1933)
Supervising Architect: James A. Wetmore. Still in use by the U.S.
District Court for the Western District of Louisiana.
Source: National Archives

In the early 1930s, two art-deco style buildings were constructed to house the growing courts in Alexandria and Monroe. The Shreveport courthouse was expanded with the addition of a fourth floor in 1931.

SECONG JUDGSEHIP CREATED
In 1938, a second judgeship was created for the Western District. The following year, in 1939, Gaston Louis Porterie, a native of Avoyelles Parish and Attorney General under Huey Long, was appointed to fill this judgeship. He had been nominated by President Franklin D. Roosevelt. Judge Porterie served until his death in 1953. For the first time in the court's history, there was now more than one judge available to travel to the various courthouses within the Western Disrtict.

Old Federal Courthouse in downtown Lafayette, served until 1999 when it was replaced. (Photo courtesy of The Morning Advocate)

In 1953, there were two judicial vacancies. Benjamin C. Dawkins, Jr. and Edwin F. Hunter, Jr. were appointed to fill these vacancies. Judge Benjamin C. Dawkins, Jr. was nominated to fill the seat vacated upon the death of his father, and served as an active judge until 1973 when he took senior status. He continued to serve the court as a senior judge until his death in 1984. Judge Edwin F. Hunter, Jr. took senior status in 1976 and served as a senior district judge in the court in the Lake Charles Division until his death in 2002. He was the longest-sitting U.S. District Court judge in the nation, having served the Western District of Louisiana for forty-eight years.

In 1960, the Lake Charles court moved into a new building which replaced its 1912 structure.

U.S. Post Office and Federal Building, Completed in 1960. Architect: Dunn Quinn The Court met here until 1994. Still used as post office.

THIRD JUDGESHIP CREATED

In 1961, Congress created a third judgeship for the Western District of Louisiana. Richard J. Putnam was appointed to this position and took senior status in 1975. Judge Putnam served until his death in 2003.

In 1967, the Western District Court discontinued use of the federal building in Opelousas to hear cases. All cases in this area were assigned to the Lafayette courthouse. The building remains today and is on the National Register of Historic Places.

FOURTH JUDGESHIP CREATED

In 1970, Congress created a fourth judgeship for this court. Nauman Steele Scott was appointed to this position in 1970. Judge Scott took senior status in 1984 and served in that capacity until his death in 2001.

In 1974, after Judge Dawkins, Jr. took senior status, Thomas

E. Stagg, Jr. was appointed as district judge. Judge Stagg
assumed senior status in 1992 and continues to serve the court
through the present time in the Shreveport Division.

In 1974, The Shreveport division of the court moved into its
new home on Fannin Street. The old building was converted
to the Shreve Memorial Library.

In 1976, after Judge Putnam took senior status, W. Eugene
Davis of Winnfield was nominated by President Gerald Ford
and was appointed district judge. He served in that capacity
in the Lafayette Division until 1983 when he was elevated to
the U. S. Fifth Circuit Court of Appeals.

In 1977, after Judge Hunter assumed senior status, Earl Ernest
Veron was appointed to the position of district judge. Judge
Veron served in the Lake Charles Division until his death in
1990.

FIFTH JUDGESHIP
In 1978, Congress created the fifth judgeship for the Western
District of Louisiana. John Malach Shaw was appointed
district judge in 1979 and served as an active judge until 1996
when he took senior status. Judge Shaw served the court as a
senior judge in the Lafayette/Opelousas Division until his
death in 1999.

SIXTH JUDGESHIP
In 1984, Congress added a sixth judgeship to the Western
District of Louisiana. In 1985, Donald E. Walter was
appointed to this new judgeship. Judge Walter served as an
active judge of this court until 2001, when he took senior
status. Judge Walter continues to serve as a senior judge in
the Shreveport Division.

In 1984, when Judge Davis was appointed to the Fifth Circuit
Court of Appeals, John M. Duhe, Jr. was appointed to fill the
judicial vacancy. Judge Duhe served on the court in the
Lafayette Division until he too was elevated to the Fifth
Circuit Court of Appeals in 1988.

Also in 1984, when Judge Scott took senior status, F. A.
Little, Jr. was appointed as district judge. Judge Little served
the court as an active judge at the Alexandria Division until
2002. He served the court as a senior judge from 2002
through 2006 when he retired.

In 1991, when Judge Duhe went to the Fifth Circuit Court of
Appeals, Richard T. Haik was selected to fill the
vacancy. Judge Haik continues to serve on the court in the
Lafayette Division.

Also in 1991, James T. Trimble, Jr. was selected to fill the
vacancy created by Judge Veron's death. Judge Trimble was
the first magistrate judge in this district to be elevated to the
position of district judge. Judge Trimble served the court in
the Lake Charles Division.

In 1994, the Lake Charles division of the court moved into its
present home, the Edwin F. Hunter Jr. building, on Broad
Street.

In 2002, Judge Trimble took senior status and serves the court
in that capacity at the present time.

SEVENTH JUDGESHIP
In 1990, Congress created a seventh judgeship for the
Western District of Louisiana. Rebecca F. Doherty was
appointed to fill this position in 1991. Judge Doherty, who is
the first woman to serve on the court, is **still in active service
with the court at the Lafayette Division.**

In 1994, Tucker L. Melançon of Avoyelles Parish was
appointed under the President Bill Clinton administration to
fill the vacancy resulting from Judge Stagg taking senior
status. Judge Melançon took senior status in 2009 and serves
the court in that capacity at the present time in the Lafayette
Division.

Edwin Hunter Federal Buidling, Lake Charles

In 1994, the court in Lake Charles moved to the Edwin F. Hunter Federal Building which was completed that year on Broad Street.

Federal Courthouse in Lafayette. (Lemoine Company, Contractors.) Completed: March, 1999 Final Contract Amount: $28,029,521 263,000 sq. ft., five story. U.S. Courthouse in downtown Lafayette, Louisiana.

In 1998, the vacancy created by the assumption of senior

status of Judge Shaw was filled by Robert G. James. Judge James continues to serve as a district judge in the Monroe Division.

In 1999, a new courthouse was constructed for the Western District in Lafayette.

In 2003, three vacancies resulting from Judges Walter, Little and Trimble taking senior status were filled. Judge Dee. D. Drell was appointed to serve in the Alexandria Division; Judge Patricia H. Minaldi was appointed to serve in the Lake Charles Division and Judge Maurice Hicks was appointed to serve in the Shreveport Division. **All three judges continue to serve the court at those locations.**

***Present Federal Courthouse, Shreveport (http://
www.lawd.uscourts.gov)***

In 2010, Judge Elizabeth E. Foote was appointed in the Shreveport Division to fill the vacancy resulting from Judge Melançon taking senior status. Judge Foote continues to serve the court at the present time.

CHIEF JUDGES
In 1949, Congress created the position of chief judge of the district court. The chief judges who have served in this district are:
        Judge Benjamin C. Dawkins, Sr. (1949-1953)
        Benjamin C. Dawkins, Jr. (1953-1973)
        Judge Edwin F. Hunter, Jr. (1973-1976)
        Judge Nauman S. Scott (1976-1984)

Judge Tom Stagg, (1984-1991)
Judge John M. Shaw (1991-1996)
Judge F. A. Little, Jr. (1996-2002)
Judge Richard T. Haik (2002-2009)
Judge Robert G. James (2009 - 2012)
Judge Dee D. Drell (2012 - Present).

DIVISIONS
The Western District of Louisiana presently consists of 42 of
the 64 parishes in Louisiana. Until 1984, the district consisted
of six statutory divisions, named for the six authorized places
of holding court, to wit: Alexandria, Lafayette, Lake Charles,
Monroe, Opelousas and Shreveport. In 1984, at the request of
the court, Congress abolished statutory divisions in the
Western District of Louisiana, but retained the authorized
places of holding court.

Today, the court is divided into five administrative divisions:
Alexandria, Lafayette, Lake Charles, Monroe, and
Shreveport. These divisions are set by vote of the authorized
judges in the court.

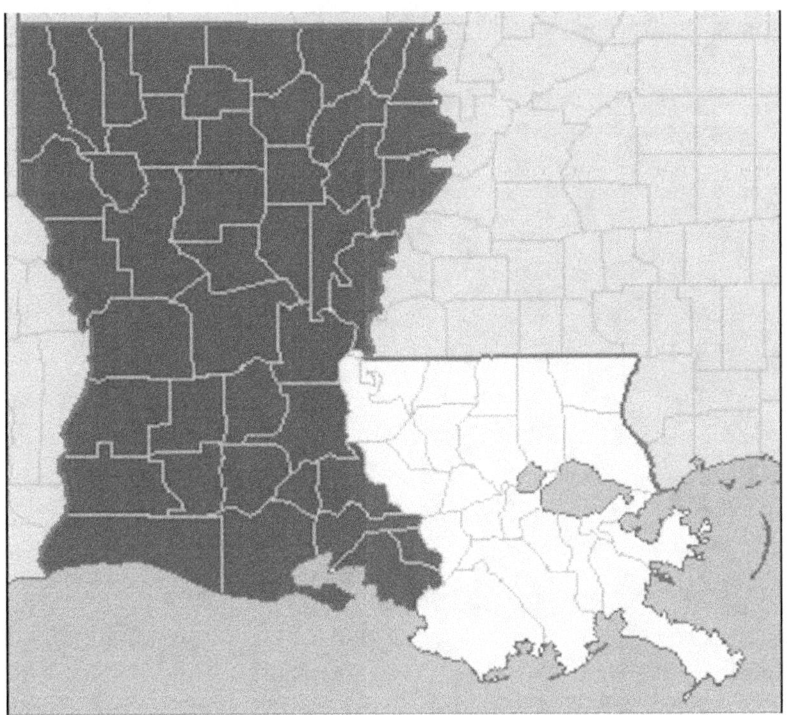

The U. S. Western District Court of Louisiana (Shaded)

Section II

The Judges
of the
U. S. Western District of
Louisiana

Hall, Dominic Augustin *Served 1804-1820*
Nominated by President Thomas Jefferson

Dick, John *Served 1821-182*
Nominated by President James Monroe

Robertson, Thomas Bolling, *Served 1824-1828*
Nominated by President James Monroe

Harper, Samuel Hadden, *Served 1829-1837*
Nominated by President Andrew Jackson

McCaleb, Theodore Howard, *Served 1841-1845*
Nominated by President John Tyler

Boyce, Henry, *Served 1849-1861*
Nominated by President Zachary Taylor

Durell, Edward Henry
Nominated by President Abraham Lincoln

Billings, Edward Coke, *Served 1876-1881*
Nominated by President Ulysses Grant

Boarman, Alexander, *Served 1881-1916*
Nominated by President James A. Garfield

Jack, George Whitfield, *Served 1917-1924*
Nominated by President Woodrow Wilson

Dawkins, Benjamin Cornwell Sr.,
Served 1924-53
Nominated by President Calvin Coolidge

Porterie, Gaston Louis Noel, *Served 1939-1954*
Nominated by President Franklin Roosevelt

Dawkins, Benjamin Cornwell Jr.,
Served 1953-1984
Nominated by President Dwight D. Eisenhower

Hunter, Edwin Ford Jr., *Served 1953-2002*
Nominated by President Dwight Eisenhower

Putnam, Richard Johnson, *Served 1961-2002*
Nominated by President John F. Kennedy

Scott, Nauman Steele, *Served 1970-2001*
Nominated by President Richard M. Nixon

Stagg, Thomas E. Jr., *Serving since 1974*
Nominated by President Richard M. Nixon

Davis, W. Eugene, *Served 1976-1983*
Nominated by President Ronald Reagan

Shaw, John Malach, *Served 1979-1999*
Nominated by President Jimmy Carter

Duhe, John Malcolm Jr., *Served 1984-1988*
Nominated by President Ronald Reagan

Little, F. A. Jr., *Served 1984-2002*
Nominated by President Ronald Reagan

Walter, Donald Ellsworth, *Serving since 1985*
Nominated by President Ronald Reagan

Haik, Richard T., *Serving since 1991*
Nominated by President George H. W. Bush

Trimble, James Travis Jr., *Serving since 1991*
Noninated by President George H. W. Bush

Doherty, Rebecca F., *Serving since 1991*
Nominated by President George H. W. Bush

Melancon, Tucker L., *Serving since 1993*
Nominated by President William J. Clinton

James, Robert Gillespie, *Serving since 1998*
Nominated by President William J. Clinton

Drell, Dee D., *serving since 2003*
Nominated by President George W. Bush

Minaldi, Patricia Head, *Serving since 2003*
Nominated by President George W. Bush

Foote, Elizabeth Erny, *Serving since 2010*
Noninated by President Barack Obama

Justice Hall

Archives of Federal Judge, Eastern District of Louisiana
(NOTE CONFLICT: This same portrait identified as Justice Strawbidge in Supreme
Court Archives.)

Hall, Dominic Augustin *Served 1804-1820*
Nominated by President Thomas Jefferson

Born January 1, 1765, SC
Died December 19, 1820, in New Orleans, LA

Federal Judicial Service:
Judge, U.S. Circuit Court for the Fifth Circuit
Received a recess appointment from Thomas Jefferson on
July 1, 1801, to a new seat authorized by 2 Stat. 89;
nominated to the same position by Thomas Jefferson on
January 6, 1802. Confirmed by the Senate on January 26,
1802, and received commission on January 26, 1802. Service
terminated on July 1, 1802, due to abolition of the court.

Judge, U.S. District Court, District of Orleans
Nominated by Thomas Jefferson on November 30, 1804, to a
new seat authorized by 2 Stat. 283. Confirmed by the Senate
on November 30, 1804, and received commission on
December 11, 1804. Service terminated on April 30, 1812,
due to abolition of the court.

Judge, U.S. District Court, District of Louisiana
Nominated by James Madison on May 27, 1812, to a new seat
authorized by 2 Stat. 701. Confirmed by the Senate on May
28, 1812, and received commission on June 1, 1812. Service
terminated on February 22, 1813, due to resignation.

Judge, U.S. District Court, District of Louisiana
Nominated by James Madison on May 29, 1813, to a seat
vacated by Dominic Hall. Confirmed by the Senate on June 1,
1813, and received commission on June 1, 1813. Service
terminated on December 19, 1820, due to death.

Professional Career:
Private practice, Charleston, South Carolina, 1789-
Judge, Louisiana Supreme Court, February-May, 1813

Dick, John *Served 1821-182*
Nominated by President James Monroe

Born 1788 in County Tyrone, Ireland
Died April 23, 1824, in New Orleans, LA

Federal Judicial Service:
Judge, U.S. District Court, District of Louisiana
Nominated by James Monroe on March 2, 1821, to a seat
vacated by Dominic A. Hall. Confirmed by the Senate on
March 2, 1821, and received commission on March 2, 1821.
Service terminated on March 3, 1823, due to reassignment.

Judge, U.S. District Court, Western District of Louisiana
Reassigned on March 3, 1823, to a new seat authorized by 3
Stat. 774. Service terminated on April 23, 1824, due to death.

Judge, U.S. District Court, Eastern District of Louisiana
Reassigned on March 3, 1823, to a new seat authorized by 3
Stat. 774. Service terminated on April 23, 1824, due to death.

Education:
Read law, 1811
Professional Career:
Private practice, New Orleans, Louisiana, 1812-1815
U.S. attorney for the Eastern District of Louisiana,
1815-1821''

Judge Bolling

Robertson, Thomas Bolling, *Served 1824-1828*
Nominated by President James Monroe

Born February 27, 1779, in Petersburg, VA
Died October 5, 1828, in White Sulphur Springs, VA (now
WV)

Federal Judicial Service:
Judge, U.S. District Court, Western District of Louisiana
Nominated by James Monroe on May 24, 1824, to a seat
vacated by John Dick. Confirmed by the Senate on May 26,
1824, and received commission on May 26, 1824. Service
terminated on October 5, 1828, due to death.

Judge, U.S. District Court, Eastern District of Louisiana
Nominated by James Monroe on May 24, 1824, to a seat
vacated by John Dick. Confirmed by the Senate on May 26,
1824, and received commission on May 26, 1824. Service
terminated on October 5, 1828, due to death.

Education:
College of William and Mary
Read law, 1806

Professional Career:
Private practice, Petersburg, Virginia, 1806
Attorney general, Orleans Territory, 1806-1807
Secretary, Louisiana Territory, 1807-1811
U.S. representative from Louisiana, 1812-1818
Private practice, Louisiana, 1818-1820
Governor, Louisiana, 1820-1822
Attorney general, State of Louisiana, 1822

Harper, Samuel Hadden, *Served 1829-1837*
Nominated by President Andrew Jackson

Born 1783 in Augusta County, VA
Died July 19, 1837, in Madisonville, LA

Federal Judicial Service:
Judge, U.S. District Court, Western District of Louisiana
Nominated by Andrew Jackson on March 6, 1829, to a seat
vacated by Thomas B. Robertson. Confirmed by the Senate
on March 7, 1829, and received commission on March 7,
1829. Service terminated on July 19, 1837, due to death.

Judge, U.S. District Court, Eastern District of Louisiana
Nominated by Andrew Jackson on March 6, 1829, to a seat
vacated by Thomas B. Robertson. Confirmed by the Senate
on March 7, 1829, and received commission on March 7,
1829. Service terminated on July 19, 1837, due to death.

Professional Career:
Private practice, New Orleans, Louisiana, 1808-1829
U.S. Army, War of 1812
State representative, Louisiana, 1814
Registrar in land office, Eastern District of Louisiana,
1821-1824
Clerk, U.S. District Court, Eastern District of Louisiana
City councilman, New Orleans, Louisiana, 1825-

Portrait provided by the Supreme Court of Louisiana

Judge McCaleb

McCaleb, Theodore Howard, *Served 1841-1845*
Nominated by President John Tyler

Born February 10, 1810, in Claiborne County, MS
Died April 29, 1864, in Claiborne County, MS

Federal Judicial Service:
Judge, U.S. District Court, Western District of Louisiana
Nominated by John Tyler on September 1, 1841, to a seat
vacated by Philip K. Lawrence. Confirmed by the Senate on
September 3, 1841, and received commission on September
3, 1841. Service terminated on February 13, 1845, due to
reassignment.

Judge, U.S. District Court, Eastern District of Louisiana
Nominated by John Tyler on September 1, 1841, to a seat
vacated by Philip K. Lawrence. Confirmed by the Senate on
September 3, 1841, and received commission on September
3, 1841. Service terminated on February 13, 1845, due to
reassignment.

Judge, U.S. District Court, District of Louisiana
Reassigned on February 13, 1845, to a new seat authorized by
5 Stat. 772. Service terminated on March 3, 1849, due to
reassignment.

Judge, U.S. District Court, Eastern District of Louisiana
Reassigned on March 3, 1849, to a new seat authorized by 90
Stat. 401. Service terminated on January 28, 1861, due to
resignation.

Education:
Yale College
Read law, 1832

Professional Career:
Private practice, New Orleans, Louisiana, 1832-1841,
1861-1864
Faculty, University of Louisiana, 1847-1864; professor,
1847-1864; dean of faculty, 1850-1862

Judge Boyce

Boyce, Henry, *Served 1849-1861*
Nominated by President Zachary Taylor

Born 1797 in Londonderry, Ireland
Died March 1, 1873, in Boyce, Rapides Parish, LA
(Town of Boyce was established on his plantation.)

Federal Judicial Service:
Judge, U.S. District Court, Western District of Louisiana
Received a recess appointment from Zachary Taylor on May
9, 1849, to a new seat authorized by 9 Stat. 401; nominated to
the same position by Zachary Taylor on December 21, 1849.
Confirmed by the Senate on August 2, 1850, and received
commission on August 2, 1850. Service terminated on
February 19, 1861, due to resignation.

Education:
Read law, 1820

Professional Career:
Private practice, Bayou Leche, Louisiana, -1824
Private practice, Alexandria, Louisiana, 1824-1828
Planter, Rapides Parish, Louisiana, 1828-1849, 1861-1873
Judge, Louisiana District Court, Sixth and Seventh Judicial
Districts, 1834-1839
U.S. attorney for the Western District of Louisiana, 1849
State legislator, Louisiana, 1865

Elected to U.S. Senate from Louisiana in 1865; U.S. Senate
refused to seat him

 HON. EDWARD H. DURELL, OF LOUISIANA.

Judge Henry

Durell, Edward Henry
Nominated by President Abraham Lincoln

Born July 14, 1810, in Portsmouth, NH
Died March 29, 1887, in Schoharie, NY

Federal Judicial Service:
Judge, U.S. District Court, Eastern District of Louisiana
Received a recess appointment from Abraham Lincoln on
May 20, 1863, to a seat vacated by Theodore McCaleb;
nominated to the same position by Abraham Lincoln on
February 8, 1864. Confirmed by the Senate on February 17,
1864, and received commission on February 17, 1864.
Service terminated on July 27, 1866, due to reassignment.

Judge, U.S. District Court, District of Louisiana
Reassigned on July 27, 1866, to a new seat authorized by 14
Stat. 300. Service terminated on December 4, 1874, due to
resignation.

Education:
Harvard College, 1831
Read law, 1834

Professional Career:
Private practice, Pittsburgh, Mississippi, and New Orleans,
Louisiana, 1835-1854
Member, City Council, New Orleans, Louisiana, 1854
Private practice, New Orleans, Louisiana
President, Bureau of Finance, New Orleans, Louisiana,
1862-1863
Mayor, New Orleans, Louisiana, 1863
Private practice, Newburgh and Schoharie, New York,
1875-1887

Edward C. Billings

Billings, Edward Coke, *Served 1876-1881*
Nominated by President Ulysses Grant

Born December 3, 1829, in Hatfield, MA
Died December 1, 1893, in New Haven, CT

Federal Judicial Service:
Judge, U.S. District Court, District of Louisiana
Nominated by Ulysses Grant on January 10, 1876, to a seat
vacated by E.H. Durell. Confirmed by the Senate on February
10, 1876, and received commission on February 10, 1876.
Service terminated on March 3, 1881, due to reassignment.

Judge, U.S. District Court, Eastern District of Louisiana
Reassigned on March 3, 1881, to a new seat authorized by 21
Stat. 507. Service terminated on December 1, 1893, due to
death.

Education:
Yale College, 1853

Judge Boarman

Boarman, Alexander, *Served 1881-1916*
Nominated by President James A. Garfield

Born December 10, 1839, in Yazoo City, MS
Died August 30, 1916, in Loon Lake, Franklin County, NY

Federal Judicial Service:
Judge, U.S. District Court, Western District of Louisiana
Nominated by James A. Garfield on May 18, 1881, to a new
seat authorized by 21 Stat. 507. Confirmed by the Senate on
May 18, 1881, and received commission on May 18, 1881.
Service terminated on August 30, 1916, due to death.

Education:
Read law, 1860
Kentucky University (now Transylvania University), 1860

Professional Career:
Confederate Army, 1861-1865
Private practice, Shreveport, Louisiana, 1866-1868,
1873-1877
Mayor, Shreveport, Louisiana, 1866-1867
City attorney, Shreveport, Louisiana, 1868-1872
U.S. representative from Louisiana, 1872-1873
Judge, Louisiana District Court, Tenth Judicial District,
1877-1881

Judge Whitfield

Jack, George Whitfield, *Served 1917-1924*
Nominated by President Woodrow Wilson

Born November 1, 1875, in Natchitoches, LA
Died March 15, 1924, in Shreveport, LA

Federal Judicial Service:
Judge, U.S. District Court, Western District of Louisiana
Nominated by Woodrow Wilson on March 6, 1917, to a seat
vacated by Alexander Boarman. Confirmed by the Senate on
March 16, 1917, and received commission on March 16,
1917. Service terminated on March 15, 1924, due to death.

Education:
Tulane University Law School, LL.B., 1898

Professional Career:
Private practice, Shreveport, Louisiana, 1898-1910
City attorney, Shreveport, Louisiana, 1910-1913
U.S. attorney for the Western District of Louisiana,
1913-1917

Dawkins, Benjamin Cornwell Sr.,
Served 1924-53
Nominated by President Calvin Coolidge

Born July 19, 1881, in Ouachita City, LA
Died August 22, 1966

Federal Judicial Service:
Judge, U.S. District Court, Western District of Louisiana
Nominated by Calvin Coolidge on April 25, 1924, to a seat
vacated by George W. Jack. Confirmed by the Senate on May
5, 1924, and received commission on May 5, 1924. Served as
chief judge, 1948-1953. Assumed senior status on May 17,
1953. Service terminated on August 22, 1966, due to death.

Education:
Tulane University Law School, LL.B., 1906

Professional Career:
Private practice, Monroe, Louisiana, 1906-1912
Judge, Louisiana District Court, 1912-1918
Associate justice, Louisiana Supreme Court, 1918-1924

Dawkins, Benjamin Cornwell Jr.,
Served 1953-1984
Nominated by President Dwight D. Eisenhower

Born August 6, 1911, in Monroe, LA
Died August 31, 1984, in Shreveport, LA

Federal Judicial Service:
Judge, U.S. District Court, Western District of Louisiana
Nominated by Dwight D. Eisenhower on July 21, 1953, to a
seat vacated by his father, Benjamin C. Dawkins, Sr..
Confirmed by the Senate on July 31, 1953, and received
commission on August 3, 1953. Served as chief judge,
1953-1973. Assumed senior status due to certified disability
on August 6, 1973. Service terminated on August 31, 1984,
due to death.

Education:
Tulane University, B.A., 1932
Louisiana State University Law School, LL.B., 1934

Professional Career:
Private practice, Monroe, Louisiana, 1934-1935
Private practice, Shreveport, Louisiana, 1935-1953
U.S. Naval Reserve lieutenant commander, 1942-1945

Judge Porterie

Porterie, Gaston Louis Noel, *Served 1939-1954*
Nominated by President Franklin Roosevelt

Born January 22, 1885, in Mansura, LA
Died March 24, 1953

Federal Judicial Service:
Judge, U.S. District Court, Western District of Louisiana
Nominated by Franklin D. Roosevelt on January 25, 1939, to
a new seat authorized by 52 Stat. 584. Confirmed by the
Senate on February 1, 1939, and received commission on
February 9, 1939. Service terminated on March 24, 1953,
due to death.

Education:
Louisiana State University, B.S., 1904
Louisiana State University Law School, LL.B., 1915

Professional Career:
Private practice, Marksville, Louisiana, 1915-1920
District attorney, Fourteenth Judicial District, Louisiana,
1916-1920
Private practice, Avoyelles Parish, Louisiana, 1920-1932
District attorney, Avoyelles Parish, Louisiana, 1920-1932
Attorney general, State of Louisiana, 1932-1939

Hunter, Edwin Ford Jr., *Served 1953-2002*
Nominated by President Dwight Eisenhower

Born February 18, 1911, in Alexandria, LA
Died February 22, 2002, in Lake Charles, LA

Federal Judicial Service:
Judge, U.S. District Court, Western District of Louisiana
Received a recess appointment from Dwight D. Eisenhower on October
3, 1953, to a seat vacated by Gaston L. Porterie; nominated to the
same position by Dwight D. Eisenhower on January 11, 1954.
Confirmed by the Senate on February 9, 1954, and received
commission on February 10, 1954. Served as chief judge, 1973-1976.
Assumed senior status on February 19, 1976. Service terminated on
February 22, 2002, due to death. Judge Hunter was the longest-
sitting U.S. District Court judge in the nation, having served
the Western District of Louisiana for forty-eight years.

Education:
George Washington University Law School, LL.B., 1938

Professional Career:
Private practice, Springhill, Louisiana, 1938-1941
Private practice, Shreveport, Louisiana, 1941-1942,
1945-1953
U.S. Navy, 1942-1945
State representative, Louisiana, 1948-1952
Executive counsel, Gov. Robert F. Kennon, Louisiana,
1952-1953

Putnam, Richard Johnson, *Served 1961-2002*
Nominated by President John F. Kennedy

Born September 27, 1913, in Abbeville, LA
Died December 16, 2002, in Abbeville, LA

Federal Judicial Service:
Judge, U.S. District Court, Western District of Louisiana
Nominated by John F. Kennedy on September 5, 1961, to a
new seat authorized by 75 Stat. 80. Confirmed by the Senate
on September 14, 1961, and received commission on
September 18, 1961. Assumed senior status due to certified
disability on December 19, 1975. Service terminated on
December 16, 2002, due to death.

Education:
Spring Hill College, B.S., 1934
Loyola University New Orleans School of Law, LL.B., 1937

Professional Career:
Private practice, Abbeville, Louisiana, 1937-1954
U.S. Naval Reserve lieutenant, 1942-1945
District attorney, Fifteenth Judicial District, Louisiana,
1948-1954
Judge, Louisiana District Court, Fifteenth Judicial District,
1954-1961
Judge, Louisiana Court of Appeal, First Judicial Circuit,
1960-1961

Photo Unavailable

Scott, Nauman Steele, *Served 1970-2001*
Nominated by President Richard M. Nixon

Born June 15, 1916, in New Roads, LA
Died September 19, 2001, in Alexandria, LA

Federal Judicial Service:
Judge, U.S. District Court, Western District of Louisiana
Nominated by Richard M. Nixon on September 14, 1970, to a
new seat authorized by 84 Stat. 294. Confirmed by the Senate
on October 13, 1970, and received commission on October
15, 1970. Served as chief judge, 1976-1984. Assumed senior
status on December 4, 1984. Service terminated on September
19, 2001, due to death.

Professional Career:
Private practice, Alexandria, Louisiana, 1941-1942,
1946-1970
U.S. Air Force first lieutenant, 1942-1946

Judge Stagg

Stagg, Thomas E. Jr., *Serving since 1974*
Nominated by President Richard M. Nixon

Born 1923 in Shreveport, LA

Federal Judicial Service:
Judge, U.S. District Court, Western District of Louisiana
Nominated by Richard M. Nixon on February 18, 1974, to a
seat vacated by Benjamin C. Dawkins, Jr.. Confirmed by the
Senate on March 7, 1974, and received commission on March
8, 1974. Served as chief judge, 1984-1991. Assumed senior
status on February 29, 1992.

Education:
Louisiana State University, B.A., 1943
Louisiana State University Law School, LL.B., 1949

Professional Career:
U.S. Army captain, Infantry, 1943-1946
Private practice, Shreveport, Louisiana, 1949-1974
Vice-president, King Hardware Co., Louisiana, 1955-1974
President, The Abe Meyer Corporation, Shreveport,
Louisiana, 1960-1974
Managing partner, Pierremont Mall Shopping Center,
1963-1974
President, Stagg Investments, Inc., 1964-1974
Managing partner, Camellia Trading Company, 1974-

Judge Davis

Davis, W. Eugene, *Served 1976-1983*
Nominated by President Ronald Reagan

Born 1936 in Winfield, AL

Federal Judicial Service:
Judge, U.S. District Court, Western District of Louisiana
Nominated by Gerald Ford on August 5, 1976, to a seat
vacated by Richard J. Putnam. Confirmed by the Senate on
September 17, 1976, and received commission on September
21, 1976. Service terminated on December 9, 1983, due to
appointment to another judicial position.

Judge, U.S. Court of Appeals for the Fifth Circuit
Nominated by Ronald Reagan on November 1, 1983, to a seat
vacated by Robert Andrew Ainsworth, Jr.. Confirmed by the
Senate on November 15, 1983, and received commission on
November 16, 1983.

Education:
Tulane University Law School, J.D., 1960

Professional Career:
Private practice, New Orleans, Louisiana, 1960-1964
Private practice, New Iberia, Louisiana 1964-1976

Judge Veron

Shaw, John Malach, *Served 1979-1999*
Nominated by President Jimmy Carter

Born November 14, 1931, in Beaumont, TX
Died December 24, 1999, in Lafayette, LA

Federal Judicial Service:
Judge, U.S. District Court, Western District of Louisiana
Nominated by Jimmy Carter on June 5, 1979, to a new seat
authorized by 92 Stat. 1629. Confirmed by the Senate on
September 25, 1979, and received commission on September
26, 1979. Served as chief judge, 1991-1996. Assumed senior
status on November 15, 1996. Service terminated on
December 24, 1999, due to death.

Education:
Washington and Lee University, B.S., 1953
Louisiana State University Law School, J.D., 1956

Professional Career:
U.S. Army, 1956-1958
U.S. Army Reserve captain, 1958-1964
Private practice, Opelousas, Louisiana, 1958-1979

Judge Little

Little, F. A. Jr., *Served 1984-2002*
Nominated by President Ronald Reagan

Born 1936 in Minneapolis, MN

Federal Judicial Service:
Judge, U.S. District Court, Western District of Louisiana
Nominated by Ronald Reagan on September 11, 1984, to a
seat vacated by Nauman S. Scott. Confirmed by the Senate on
October 11, 1984, and received commission on October 12,
1984. Served as chief judge, 1996-2002. Assumed senior
status on May 30, 2002. Service terminated on May 15, 2006,
due to retirement.

Education:
Tulane University, B.A., 1958
Tulane University Law School, J.D., 1961

Professional Career:
Private practice, New Orleans, Louisiana, 1961-1965
Private practice, Alexandria, Louisiana, 1965-1984

Duhe, John Malcolm Jr., *Served 1984-1988*
Nominated by President Ronald Reagan

Born 1933 in Iberia Parish, LA

Federal Judicial Service:
Judge, U.S. District Court, Western District of Louisiana
Nominated by Ronald Reagan on May 15, 1984, to a seat
vacated by Eugene Davis. Confirmed by the Senate on June
8, 1984, and received commission on June 11, 1984. Service
terminated on November 9, 1988, due to appointment to
another judicial position.

Judge, U.S. Court of Appeals for the Fifth Circuit
Nominated by Ronald Reagan on June 27, 1988, to a seat
vacated by Albert Tate. Confirmed by the Senate on October
14, 1988, and received commission on October 17, 1988.
Assumed senior status on April 7, 1999.

Education:
Tulane University, B.S., 1955
Tulane University Law School, LL.B., 1957

Professional Career:
Private practice, New Iberia, Louisiana, 1957-1978
Judge, Louisiana District Court, Sixteenth Judicial District,
1979-1984

Walter, Donald Ellsworth, *Serving since 1985*
Nominated by President Ronald Reagan

Born 1936 in Jennings, LA

Federal Judicial Service:
Judge, U.S. District Court, Western District of Louisiana
Nominated by Ronald Reagan on May 15, 1985, to a new seat
authorized by 98 Stat. 333. Confirmed by the Senate on July
10, 1985, and received commission on July 11, 1985.
Assumed senior status on November 30, 2001.

Education:
Louisiana State University, B.A., 1961
Louisiana State University Law School, J.D., 1964

Professional Career:
U.S. Army, 1957-1958
Private practice, Lake Charles, Louisiana, 1964-1969
U.S. attorney for the Western District of Louisiana,
1969-1977
Private practice, Shreveport, Louisiana, 1978-1985

Judge Haik

Haik, Richard T., *Serving since 1991*
Nominated by President George H. W. Bush

Born 1950 in Lafayette, LA

Federal Judicial Service:
Judge, U.S. District Court, Western District of Louisiana
Nominated by George H.W. Bush on April 11, 1991, to a seat
vacated by John M. Duhe, Jr.. Confirmed by the Senate on
May 24, 1991, and received commission on May 30, 1991.
Served as chief judge, 2002-2009.

Education:
University of Southwestern Louisiana (now University of
Louisiana at Lafayette), B.S., 1971
Loyola University New Orleans School of Law, J.D., 1975

Professional Career:
Private practice, New Iberia, Louisiana, 1975-1984
Louisiana National Guard, 1971-1978
U.S. Army Reserve captain, 1980-1984
Judge, Louisiana District Court, 1984-1991

Judge Trimble

Trimble, James Travis Jr., *Serving since 1991*
Noninated by President George H. W. Bush

Born 1932 in Bunkie, LA

Federal Judicial Service:
Judge, U.S. District Court, Western District of Louisiana
Nominated by George H.W. Bush on June 27, 1991, to a seat
vacated by Earl E. Veron. Confirmed by the Senate on
September 12, 1991, and received commission on September
16, 1991. Assumed senior status on September 13, 2002.

U.S. Magistrate, U.S. District Court, Western District of
Louisiana, 1986-1991

Education:
Louisiana State University, B.A., 1955
Louisiana State University Law School, LL.B., 1956

Professional Career:
U.S. Air Force, JAG Corps, 1956-1959
Private practice, Alexandria, Louisiana, 1959-1986

Judge Doherty

Doherty, Rebecca F., *Serving since 1991*
Nominated by President George H. W. Bush

Born 1952 in Fort Worth, TX

Federal Judicial Service:
Judge, U.S. District Court, Western District of Louisiana
Nominated by George H.W. Bush on June 27, 1991, to a new
seat authorized by 104 Stat. 5089. Confirmed by the Senate
on October 31, 1991, and received commission on November
5, 1991.

Education:
Northwestern State University of Louisiana, B.A., 1973
Northwestern State University of Louisiana, M.A., 1975
Louisiana State University, Paul M. Hebert Law Center, J.D.,
1981

Professional Career:
Private practice, Lafayette, Louisiana, 1981-1991

Judge Melancon

Melancon, Tucker L., *Serving since 1993*
Nominated by President William J. Clinton

Born 1946 in Bryan, TX

Federal Judicial Service:
Judge, U.S. District Court, Western District of Louisiana
Nominated by William J. Clinton on November 18, 1993, to a
seat vacated by Thomas E. Stagg, Jr.. Confirmed by the
Senate on February 10, 1994, and received commission on
February 11, 1994. Assumed senior status due to certified
disability on February 14, 2009.

Education:
Louisiana State University, B.S., 1968
Tulane University Law School, J.D., 1973

Professional Career:
Private practice, Marksville, Louisiana, 1973-1993

Photo Unavailable

James, Robert Gillespie, *Serving since 1998*
Nominated by President William J. Clinton

Born 1946 in Ruston, LA

Federal Judicial Service:
Judge, U.S. District Court, Western District of Louisiana
Nominated by William J. Clinton on January 27, 1998, to a
seat vacated by John M. Shaw. Confirmed by the Senate on
July 31, 1998, and received commission on August 3, 1998.
Served as chief judge, 2009-2012.

Education:
Louisiana Tech University, B.A., 1968
Louisiana State University Law School, J.D., 1971

Professional Career:
Private practice, Ruston, Louisiana, 1971-1998
Business law instructor, Louisiana Tech University,
1992-1998
Judge, Ruston [Louisiana] City Court, 1985-1998

Judge Drell

Drell, Dee D., *serving since 2003*
Nominated by President George W. Bush

Born 1947 in New Orleans, LA

Federal Judicial Service:
Judge, U.S. District Court, Western District of Louisiana
Nominated by George W. Bush on January 15, 2003, to a seat
vacated by F.A. Little, Jr.. Confirmed by the Senate on April
9, 2003, and received commission on April 10, 2003. Served
as chief judge, 2012-present.

Education:
Tulane University, B.A., 1968
Tulane University Law School, J.D., 1971

Professional Career:
U.S. Army, JAG Corps, 1971-1975
Private practice, Louisiana, 1975-2003

Hicks, Samuel Maurice, Jr. *Serving since 2003*
Nominated by President George Bush

Born 1952 in New Orleans, Louisiana

Federal Judicial Service:
Judge, U.S. District Court, Western District of Louisiana
Nominated by President George Bush Jan. 7, 2003 to seat
vacated by Donald Walter. Confirmed by Senate May 19,
2003.

Education:
Texas Christian University, B. S. 1974
Louisiana State University Law School, 1977

Professional Career:
Law Clerck, Louisiana Legislative Council, 1975-1977

Minaldi, Patricia Head, *Serving since 2003*
Nominated by President George W. Bush

Born 1959 in Somerville, MA

Federal Judicial Service:
Judge, U.S. District Court, Western District of Louisiana
Nominated by George W. Bush on January 15, 2003, to a seat
vacated by James T. Trimble Jr.. Confirmed by the Senate on
May 6, 2003, and received commission on May 9, 2003.

Education:
Wesleyan University, B.A., 1980
Tulane University Law School, J.D., 1983

Professional Career:
Assistant district attorney, Orleans Parish, Louisiana,
1983-1986
Assistant district attorney, Calcasieu Parish, Louisiana,
1986-1996
Judge, Louisiana District Court, Fourteenth Judicial District,
1996-2003

Judge Foote

Foote, Elizabeth Erny, *Serving since 2010*
Nonimated by President Barack Obama

Born 1953 in Lafayette, LA

Federal Judicial Service:
Judge, U.S. District Court, Western District of Louisiana
Nominated by Barack Obama on February 4, 2010, to a seat
vacated by Tucker L. Melancon. Confirmed by the Senate on
June 15, 2010, and received commission on June 15, 2010.

Education:
Louisiana State University, B.A., 1974
Duke University, M.A., 1975
Louisiana State University Law School, J.D., 1978

Professional Career:
Law clerk, Hon. William Culpepper, Louisiana Court of
Appeal, Third Judicial Circuit, 1978-1979
Private practice, Alexandria, Louisiana, 1979-2010

The seven current sitting judges in the Western District are:

Chief Judge Dee D. Drell, Alexandria
Judge Richard T. Haik, Lafayette
Judge Rebecca F. Doherty, Lafayette
Lake Charles, Judge Patricia Minaldi
Monroe, Judge Robert G. James
Shreveport, Judge S. Maurice Hicks, Jr.
Judge Elizabeth Enry Foote

Federal Courthouses are located in Alexandria, Lafayette, Lake Charles, Monroe, and Shreveport.